Canaletto and Warwick Castle

Detail from *Warwick Castle: the East Front from the Courtyard* by Canaletto. (See plate 23.)

Canaletto and Warwick Castle

David Buttery

Phillimore

1992

Published by
PHILLIMORE & CO. LTD.
Shopwyke Hall, Chichester, Sussex

© David Buttery, 1992

ISBN 0 85033 828 X

Printed and bound in Great Britain by
BIDDLES LTD.
Guildford, Surrey

To the memory of my sister Maureen

Contents

List of Plates viii

Acknowledgements x

Introduction xi

1. The Artist 1
2. The Patron 7
3. Warwick 11
4. The Pictures 20
5. The Story 55

Bibliography 65

List of Subscribers 67

The Plates

1. *Portrait of Giovanni Antonio Canal, called Canaletto*, engraving by Antonio Visentini after G. B. Piazzetta. From the *Prospectus Magni Canalis Venetiarum*, 1735. 2

2. *The Bucintoro returning to the Molo, Venice*, by Canaletto, c.1732. Royal Collection. 4

3. *Portrait of Francis Greville, first Earl Brooke* by Sir Joshua Reynolds, 1755. Private Collection. 9

4. Detail of the figure of King Richard III from the Rous Roll, 1483. British Library Add. MSS. 48976. 12

5. Detail of an engraving of Warwick from the London road by Wenceslaus Hollar, published in Sir William Dugdale's *Antiquities of Warwickshire*, 1656, pp. 298-99. 14

6. *Warwick Castle from the North-east*, engraving by Samuel and Nathaniel Buck, 1729. 16

7. *Warwick Castle from the South-east*, engraving by Samuel and Nathaniel Buck, 1729. 17

8. Warwick Castle from across Castle Park, 1991. 18

9. *Warwick Castle: the South Front*, painting by Canaletto, 1748. Private Collection. 21

10. *Warwick Castle: the South Front*, painting by Canaletto, 1748. Thyssen-Bournemisza Collection, Lugano. 24

11. *Warwick Castle: the South Front*, drawing by Canaletto, 1748. Private Collection. 25

12. Hoare's Bank ledger T, folio 224 (detail). 26

13. *Warwick Castle: the South Front*, painting by Canaletto, 1748(9). Paul Mellon Collection, Upperville, Virginia. 28

14. Detail of plate 13. 29

15. A folio in the first Earl Brooke's estate account ledgers (detail). Greville Archive, Warwick County Record Office. 30

16. Voucher in Canaletto's own hand from the first Earl

Brooke's estate accounts. Greville Archive, Warwick County Record Office. 31

17. *Warwick Castle: the East Front from the Outer Court*, painting by Canaletto, 1752. Birmingham Museum and Art Gallery. 32

18 & 19. Detail of plate 17. 33

20. Warwick Castle: the south front, 1991. .... 34/5

21. Hoare's Bank ledger T, folio 224 (detail). 36

22. Hoare's Bank ledger W, folio 27 (detail). 37

23. *Warwick Castle: the East Front from the Courtyard*, painting by Canaletto, 1752. Birmingham Museum and Art Gallery. 38

24. Detail of plate 23. 39

25. Warwick Castle: the east front, 1991. 41

26. *Warwick Castle: the East Front from the Outer Court*, drawing by Canaletto, 1752. Metropolitan Museum of Art, New York, Robert Lehman Collection. 43

27. Hoare's Bank ledger W, folio 27 (detail). 44

28. Warwick Castle: the east front from the courtyard, 1991. 45

29. *Warwick Castle: the East Front from the Courtyard*, drawing by Canaletto, 1752. J. Paul Getty Museum, Malibu, California. 46

30. *St Mary's Church and Church Street, Warwick*, drawing by Canaletto, 1748 or 1752. British Museum. 47

31. Warwick Castle: the east front, 1991. .... 48/9

32. Plan of Warwick by Matthias Baker (detail), 1788. Greville Archive, Warwick County Record Office. 50

33. *The Town and Castle of Warwick seen from the Gardens of the Priory*, drawing by Canaletto, 1748 or 1752. Yale Center for British Art, New Haven, Connecticut. 51

34. St Mary's church and Church Street, Warwick, 1991. .. 52

35. Warwick town and castle from Priory Park, 1991. 53

36. *Warwick Castle: the Courtyard and Residential Apartment*, painting by John Pye, 1765. Private Collection. 56

37 & 38. Warwick Castle: the Red Room hung with Canaletto's pictures, 1950. .... 58/59

39. Signature of the first Earl Brooke. 61

40. Signature of Canaletto. 61

41. Warwick Castle: the south front, 1991. .... 62/3

Acknowledgements

Her Majesty the Queen. Four of the 10 Canaletto paintings and drawings of Warwick are in private collections: to Mr. Paul Mellon, the Thyssen-Bournemisza Collection, the two other private collectors, my sincere thanks for making this book possible. The remaining six Canalettos are held by museums: Birmingham Museum and Art Gallery, British Museum, J. Paul Getty Museum, Metropolitan Museum of Art and Yale Center for British Art. To these, again, my thanks.

A special word of gratitude to the doyen of Canaletto scholars, J. G. Links, whose friendship and generosity has made all Canaletto study worthwhile.

I am indebted to the retired archivist for Warwick, Mr. Michael Farr, his colleagues of the Warwick County Record Office, the Partners of Hoare's Bank, and their Archivist, Mrs. Victoria Moger, for assistance with my research.

For help in seeing the book produced I must thank Mr. Martin Westwood, former manager of Warwick Castle, and Mr. John Cope, chief photographer of Birmingham Museum and Art Gallery, now retired, for his excellent printing of my photographs.

Introduction

This is a story, a history, of two men and of how they came together to glorify, in their different ways, a great fragment of England's past. One of these men was from Northern Italy, a native of the Serene Republic of Venice and a scenic artist of genius who though born on the shores of the Adriatic Sea was, by virtue of his art, to come and depict scenes of England. The other, an English aristocrat, was to be born in and was to inherit an ancestral home which was not simply a family seat but, by reason of its traditions, a very part of England's history. The relationship of these two men was that of artist and patron — the one paid, the other paying — yet their association was to transcend the merely commercial by its creation of art. This art was to be a group of paintings and drawings — of pigments in oil applied to canvas by the brush in the painter's hand, of ink drawn upon paper by the pen at his fingertips. These works have now come to form a piece of the very history that artist and patron sought to portray and to dramatise. Almost two and a half centuries have passed since these pictures were created. In those years many changes have occurred, many events taken place, yet both subject and art continue to exist. The story is one of a glorious beginning, of a family tradition, and of a magnificent survival.

The Artist

> '... came to London from Venice the Famous Painter of Views Cannalletti ...'
>
> *George Vertue, 1746*

THE SCENIC PAINTER AND DRAUGHTSMAN whom we know as Canaletto [1] was born in Venice on 28 October 1697. He was given the Christian names Zuane Antonio while his surname was simply Canal. Zuane is the Venetian manner of the Italian Giovanni or, in English, John. Although Canaletto's true name was Canal he himself used other forms of it including Canale, da Canal and Canaleto, while he would also vary the use of his first names. In 18th-century England he was most commonly known as Canaletti though this may also be found spelt Cannelletti. The precise meaning of Canaletto is simply little Canal or son of Canal, and the artist probably adopted the use of this name when he was about twenty-five to distinguish himself from his father, Bernardo, who was to live until 1744. It is now the name by which he is universally known.

Canaletto's father, Bernardo Canal, was a designer and painter of scenery for the theatre and for opera while the Canal family itself, which may be traced back to the 15th century, belonged to the minor Venetian nobility and enjoyed the right to a coat of arms. Of the artist's early years and training we know nothing, but, almost certainly, he began his artistic life assisting his father in the work of scene painting for the stage. We do know that in 1719 he was engaged, with his father, in this activity at Rome. The following year he returned to Venice and six years later he was engaged upon paintings commissioned for the second Duke of Richmond by the Irish impresario and agent, Owen McSwiney. This is the first we know of what was to be a feature of Canaletto's life, the demand for his work by English collectors.

The beginning of this involvement with England came shortly after Canaletto had abandoned the painting of scenery as a career and had begun painting pictures of the city of Venice itself. Though he is by far the most famous artist to depict Venice, it should not be thought that Canaletto was the first such painter to do so. Venice had, in fact, been depicted in paintings as early as the 15th century. Canaletto was himself influenced by the work of his fellow Venetian painter, Luca Carlevaris, then the principal portrayer of views of the city and its elaborate public ceremonies. Carlevaris was 32 years older than Canaletto, and his work lacks the animation and brilliance of lighting which the younger artist

1. *Giovanni Antonio Canal called Canaletto* (1697-1768), engraving by Antonio Visentini after G. B. Piazzetta, 1735.

The Artist

was to achieve. Canaletto's depictions of his native city had, by 1725, already brought him recognition, since in that year he painted pictures for a rich Italian cloth merchant from Lucca, Stefano Conti. As his agent Conti employed a minor painter, Alessandro Marchesini, who wrote that Canaletto's scintillating use of light was dazzling everyone who saw his work. Thus by the middle of the 1720s, Canaletto had established his first links with England and, by his brilliance, made himself the leading painter in the form of art which was to bring him fame — scenes of La Serenissima — the city of Venice [2].

The patronage of Canaletto by the English, which had begun in 1726, was to continue throughout the 1720s and '30s. This was the era of the Grand Tour, that progression around Europe indulged in by young noblemen and considered an essential part of their education. Needless to say Italy and, in particular, Rome, with its Classical and Renaissance associations, was the climax of this experience. The origins of Venice did not lie in the ancient world and, though it had once been a powerful city with an empire in the eastern Mediterranean, by Canaletto's time this had been lost. The Venice of the 18th-century Englishman on the Tour was one of sensuality and pleasure with its carnivals, theatres, cafés, casinos and courtesans — things that the tourist helped to finance. Thus if Rome represented the cultural summit of the Tour, then Venice was its triumph of pleasure. Naturally the English visiting Venice wished to acquire a painting of this beautiful and fascinating city to record their visit and this Canaletto was the perfect artist to provide.

Owen McSwiney had been Canaletto's first agent in his dealings with English patrons, but by the end of the 1720s Canaletto had found another and a far more useful one. This was the merchant, banker, collector, and ultimately British Consul at Venice, Joseph Smith. With the assistance of Smith, Canaletto built up a lucrative practice, and there may have been an agreement between them that Smith sold pictures in return for a commission. By dealing with Smith, collectors in England were able to order pictures without having to visit Venice itself. In addition, Smith acquired many works by Canaletto for his own collection, which included paintings, drawings and etchings. He was to be not merely an agent and patron but also a friend to the artist.

With Joseph Smith acting for him, Canaletto's work was in great demand throughout the 1720s and '30s. He was, however, not an easy man to have dealings with. In 1727 McSwiney wrote of him:

> The fellow is whimsical and vary's [sic] his prices, every day; and he that has a mind to have any of his work, must not seem to be too fond of it, for he'l be ye worse treated for it, both in price and the painting too. He has more work than he can doe in any reasonable time and well ...

The Artist

Travellers from all over Europe were visiting Venice and, falling under its spell, longed to preserve a memory of it; no one could resolve this longing as completely as Canaletto. The greatest number of these visitors were from England, and by 1739 it was said that he was being treated with such generosity by them — paying three times his normal price for a painting — that no others could do business with him. Clearly Canaletto knew very well the quality and value of his work, and the ability of his patrons to afford to pay for the paintings which he alone could create. It was this which caused both McSwiney and Smith to write that he was covetous and greedy and that 'he is so much followed and all are so ready to pay him his own price for his work'.

The reasons for Canaletto's great success certainly lay partly in the simple wish his clients had for views of Venice and, in this sense, his art met a precise demand of the market. The deeper reason for his achievement lay in his ability to dramatise and to create an image of the city swept by the golden light the tourists wished to remember. Canaletto's paintings and drawings were created in his studio from sketches made of the buildings and canals of Venice. Once in the studio he would change the sizes of buildings, the positions, and alter the perspective of a scene. Essentially his skill lay in using the pictorial possibilities of a view or scene to dramatic effect in the actual work of art. In this way certain of Canaletto's works are more closely related to reality than others. There was for him a distinction between what he called 'veduta essatta' or 'veduta dal naturale' (accurate views of actual places) and 'veduta ideate' (imaginary or ideal views). In his works known as capriccios, which he executed in his later years, this concept of the ideal is total, with the view being entirely imaginary, though possibly incorporating elements of reality such as buildings he had seen or sketched. In his depictions of actual places, Canaletto was always willing to improve on reality if this would result in a finer painting or drawing. Canaletto was, in short, an artist who always held elements of reality and artistic creativity in balance. It was his ability to do this which makes him a great painter and explains the success of his work.

The years 1730-40 were the period of Canaletto's greatest success, and most of his major depictions of Venice were produced at this time. Amongst the members of the English aristocracy to acquire Canaletto's paintings were the Dukes of Bedford, Leeds and Kent, the Earls of Carlisle and Fitzwilliam, and the Countess of Essex. Many of these collections have suffered losses over the centuries, but the pictures bought by the fourth Duke of Bedford may still be seen at Woburn Abbey. It is possible that the first Earl Brooke of Warwick Castle, who was to be a leading patron of Canaletto when the artist came to England, also

2. Canaletto, *Venice: The Bucintoro returning to the Molo on Ascension Day*, c.1732. Oil on canvas, 76.8 x 125.4 cm. Royal Collection.

acquired views of Venice by him. His aunt, Lady Hertford, wrote that this was so, but unfortunately, if he did possess such pictures, they have never been identified.

In the early 1740s the great period of Canaletto's portrayal of Venice came to a close. The demand amongst English clients for views of the city had been satisfied, and perhaps the artist had tired of painting picture after picture of Venice. In 1741 the War of the Austrian Succession had broken out, and the following year fighting spread to Italy. This reduced trade between England and Venice and also made it unlikely that English tourists would visit the city, as the engraver and antiquary George Vertue noted: 'of late few persons travel to Italy from hence during the wars'. At this time Canaletto painted less and devoted himself to etching and drawing. In particular he developed the latter as an independent work of art, something which was to continue when he came to England.

Canaletto should have earned much when his work was in great demand, but the sudden falling off in business left him with only one patron, Joseph Smith. This exhaustion of, and interruption in, the market for his previous work must have presented him with a problem. It may have been Smith who suggested that he should follow in the footsteps of other Venetian artists and come to England as a solution to his difficulties. One such artist was Jacapo Amigoni and Canaletto may have acted upon his recommendation. Very probably he believed that since the English clients had been his principal as well as his most generous patrons, he could hope to do well in their country. Whatever the precise circumstances which motivated his decision, in the spring of 1746 Canaletto left his native city of Venice and set out for London.

The Patron

'The castle ... now belongs to Earl Brooke ... who has greatly beautifyed the park and the whole place by plantations.'
Richard Pococke, 1757

THROUGHOUT HISTORY the artist has required some source of finance, of payment, in order that he may practise his skill, his art. There has, therefore, always been an unbreakable link between the creation of art and the possession of wealth. In the 19th century there arose the vision of the artist as an heroic individual who lived for his art alone and who could survive by selling his 'masterpieces' to those willing and able to afford them. This is still many people's conception of the artist today. The reality of the life of the artist is that he must, within the society in which he lives, find those willing to pay him for his work. Such individuals will themselves form a part of some definable group within a society. Thus the Roman Catholic Church and, in particular, certain of its members financed many of the great works which we think of as the art of the Italian Renaissance. Other societies, arising in different countries and at different times, have developed other classes, other institutions, which have had the wish to employ artists. In this sense, works of art have always been the prize of the winner in the game of life.

Though there were the beginnings of bourgeois patronage in 18th-century England, the predominant employers of the artist remained the aristocracy. There continued, therefore, that relationship between artists and the country's great aristocratic families. One member of such a family was Francis Greville, eighth Baron Brooke, first Earl Brooke and first Earl of Warwick [3]. He was to be a leading patron of Canaletto during the artist's years in England.

The Greville family's ancestral home had, since the 17th century, been the castle of Warwick. The origins of the Grevilles, however, go back to the 14th century and to the Gloucestershire village of Chipping Campden. At Campden the Grevilles had prospered in the wool trade, and in 1398 William Greville bought an estate in Warwickshire. At this time Warwick Castle was held by the Beauchamp family and the Grevilles did not take possession of it for another 206 years. During these two centuries, succeeding generations of the family lived first at Milcote Manor and, subquently, at Beauchamp's Court, near Alcester, and Wedgnock

Park at Warwick. These last two houses were abandoned in the years following James I's granting of Warwick Castle to Sir Fulke Greville in 1604.

Sir Fulke Greville, first Lord Brooke, is perhaps the best known of all the Grevilles. A poet and courtier in the reign of Elizabeth I, he declared himself the Queen's servant and probably owned a portrait of her in her coronation robes. He also owned a painting of a school friend whose life was thought to embody the quintessence of knightly virtue, Sir Philip Sidney. Sir Fulke was to write a life of Sidney and to hold the office of Chancellor of the Exchequer under King James who, in 1621, conferred upon him the title of Baron Brooke. He was not, however, to meet a peaceful end, being murdered at his London house by his servant in 1628.

The first Baron Brooke never married and was succeeded in the title and in the ownership of Warwick Castle by his cousin, Robert Greville, who was himself to meet a violent death. As one of England's leading Parliamentarians he opposed Charles I in the Civil War and helped bring success at the Battle of Edgehill in 1642. A year later he was killed during the siege of Lichfield.

The following five Barons Brooke made little impression on history though the fourth Baron, Robert, did play a part in the Restoration of Charles II and was responsible for remodelling the interiors of Warwick Castle. It is not until the birth of Francis Greville in 1719, and his succession as the eighth Baron Brooke eight years later, that we come upon a member of the Greville family who was to be a significant patron of the arts.

Francis Greville's father, William Greville, seventh Baron Brooke, had, in 1711, been described as: 'A young debauched and rakish man'. He was then some 17 years of age and this description may account for his early death at the age of thirty-three. In 1716 the seventh Baron had married Mary Thynne, granddaughter of the first Viscount Weymouth, and Francis Greville was to be their only surviving child, as Mary died the year after he was born. The death of his mother, followed by that of his father only seven years later, left him an orphan at the age of eight; he was then brought up by his mother's sister, Frances, who was the wife of Algernon Seymour, Earl of Hertford. He must have been a sickly child since he suffered from a congenital disease which restricted his growth; thus, years later, Horace Walpole was to refer to him frequently as 'little Brook'. The year after he succeeded to the Barony of Brooke and the ownership of Warwick Castle, 1728, Francis Greville was sent for schooling to Winchester College, where he was a pupil until 1734. A portrait of him still hangs there.

In 1735 Francis Greville, Lord Brooke, set out on his Grand Tour in the company of his tutor, Robert Symner. He was to be abroad for some five years. His precise movements on the continent are not known, but almost certainly most of his time was spent in Italy, the visiting of which was the real purpose of the Tour. Brooke's actual journeyings within Italy are, again,

uncertain, but he definitely saw Rome, as he wrote of being disappointed by the city, though not by St Peter's Basilica. We know, too, that he admired the cascades at Terni, in the Umbria district of central Italy, and that he also visited Florence, as he spoke of seeing a man killed in a horse race there. The other great Italian city normally visited by those on tour was Venice, but whether Brooke saw it or whether his poor health forced him to omit it from his itinerary we cannot be sure. As his aunt, Lady Hertford, was to write: 'Lord Brooke was so ill all the time he was in Italy, that he took little delight in anything he saw there; nor could he see half of what he intended'. Lady Hertford also states that Brooke possessed views of Venice by Canaletto, which implies that he did indeed visit the city.

Lord Brooke returned from Italy by way of Switzerland and France, spending time in both Geneva and Paris. He remained long enough in the French capital to sit for a portrait, and arrived back in London in the spring of 1740. The year of the conclusion of his Grand Tour was that in which Brooke came of age and this, no doubt, was partly the reason for his return. In the event, Brooke's coming into possession of Warwick Castle and its estates was not to be a peaceful affair. He discovered, much to his chagrin, that his trustees had neglected their duties to such a degree that he was compelled to resort to the law in an attempt to recover his inheritance.

3. Sir Joshua Reynolds (1723-92), *Portrait of Francis Greville, first Earl Brooke*, 1755. Oil on canvas, 90.2 x 68.6 cm. Private Collection.

The years immediately following Lord Brooke's return to England also witnessed his marriage, in May 1742, to Elizabeth Hamilton, a daughter of Lord Archibald Hamilton, who was the youngest son of the third Duke of Hamilton. She was almost the same age as Brooke and was, if Horace Walpole may be believed, equally as small, since he described her as 'excessively pretty and sensible, but as diminutive as he'. This marriage was to have historical consequences, as Elizabeth Hamilton's brother, William, later Sir William, was to be British Ambassador at Naples. It was this family connection which resulted in Brooke's eldest son, George Greville, acquiring from Sir William what became known as the Warwick Vase, while Brooke's second son, Charles, dispatched his mistress, Emily Hart, to Sir William. She thus became Lady Hamilton and, in due course, met Nelson.

As Lord Brooke's trustees had neglected the collection of the income from his estates, they had also very probably failed to maintain Warwick Castle, its gardens and park. In any case, both the style of earlier changes to the building, and the character of the 17th-century formal gardens, must have seemed outdated to Brooke. Accordingly, in the 1740s he began a series of major works at Warwick which were to continue for the rest of his life. These commenced in 1744, when he extended the castle grounds by acquiring land belonging to the town of Warwick. Four years later, in 1748, he began to employ Lancelot 'Capability' Brown as both architect and landscape gardener. Brooke was one of the great gardener's first patrons and clearly had a high regard for him, as during 1757 he was one of the group of aristocrats who pressed for him to receive a royal appointment, which was finally granted in 1764. In all, Brown was employed at Warwick Castle for some 13 years. We know this because of the payments to him from Brooke's bank account.

Lord Brooke took great pride in his ownership of Warwick. On three occasions he was portrayed with the plans of his schemes for its improvement, and it is not surprising that he wished for depictions of the castle itself. With paintings and drawings, which he could keep in his London house to show his friends, he could display not only his family seat but also his patronage of the artist who had served him. Brooke had spent his childhood in the company of his aunt's daughter, Elizabeth, who in 1740 married Sir Hugh Smithson, later to be the first Duke of Northumberland. Smithson was Canaletto's first important patron when the artist arrived in England and it was almost certainly he who introduced Canaletto to Brooke. Thus at the time when Brooke was engaged upon his works at the castle there was, newly arrived in England, the very artist to portray Warwick for him.

Warwick

> 'Here is a castle strong both by Art and nature.'
> *George Beaumont and Henry Disney, 1768*

THE TOWN OF WARWICK (its name meaning a dwelling by a weir or crossing point in a river) dates from Anglo-Saxon times and may have been first settled in the sixth century. In 914 King Alfred the Great's daughter, Ethelfleda, constructed a fort at Warwick, the first defensive structure built to overlook the habitation by the River Avon. Almost certainly due to its central position, Warwick became an administrative centre for the shire during the 10th century. Thus it was natural that when William the Conqueror embarked upon his great scheme of castle-building to secure his hold on England, following his victory over King Harold at the battle of Hastings, he should have placed one at Warwick. The sandstone cliff formed by the action of the Avon and the presence of the river itself made it a perfect site for a castle with its obvious natural defences.

The building of Warwick Castle began in 1068 and this original structure would have been of the motte-and-bailey type. This early form of castle consisted of an earth mound or motte surrounded by a ditch, and beyond this one or more baileys or courtyards, each again surrounded by a ditch. On the summit of the motte, which could itself have been fenced, would be a wooden tower or building. Later this was often replaced by a stone structure. Thus there has been a castle at Warwick, on the present site, for some nine hundred years, though of William the Conqueror's building only the mound survives. It was to be from these early Norman beginnings that the present castle began slowly to evolve, firstly by the construction of a stone tower at the base of the mound and then, by progressive stages of building, northward along the stone bluff above the Avon.

The first family to be Earls of Warwick was that of de Beaumont, who received the title from William II in 1088. The King's father, the Conqueror, had previously granted the family custody of the castle. The male line of the de Beaumonts died out in the 13th century and they were succeeded at Warwick by the family of Maudit which, in turn, gave way in 1268 to that of Beauchamp. The Beauchamps were to build at Warwick on a grand scale and, even after 600 years, they are still responsible for

Canaletto and Warwick Castle

the essential appearance of the castle today.

The first Beauchamp Earl of Warwick was William, whose son Guy, the 'Black Hound of Arden', is best remembered for his role in the seizing and putting to death of Piers Gaveston, favourite of Edward II. Guy Beauchamp's son, Thomas, succeeded to the earldom and the ownership of the castle at the age of only two. It was he who was to build, in the middle of the 14th century, the great east front of Warwick with its two majestic towers and its central gatehouse and barbican. Thomas Beauchamp fought in the Hundred Years War against France, seeing service at the battles of Crécy and Poitiers. It may be that something of the element of fantasy, which is implicit in the high towers he built at Warwick, owes its origins to the castles he had seen while on campaign in France. He died in 1369 and was succeeded by his second son, another Thomas, who continued his father's glorification of the castle. He completed the work of building the towers of the east front and extended the living quarters, creating a new and larger hall. This hall, though many times altered and rebuilt, still survives on its original site.

The last Beauchamp Earl of Warwick died in 1446 and the earldom and ownership of Warwick Castle then devolved, through his daughter, Anne, to her husband, Richard Neville, who became famous under the sobriquet of 'the Kingmaker'. Neville

4. Detail of the figure of King Richard III from the Rous Roll, a history of the Earls of Warwick, by John Rous (c.1411-91), with illuminations by an unknown artist, 1483. British Library.

was immensely rich, not merely through his estates but also by reason of the high offices of state he held under the Crown. Consequently he was able to live at Warwick in great style. He was, however, involved in that dynastic struggle between the Houses of Lancaster and York known as the Wars of the Roses, and fell at the Battle of Barnet in 1471. Seven years later, in 1478, the castle came under royal control and it is at about this time that we may catch our first glimpse of its appearance [4]. There is a drawing, by an anonymous English or Flemish artist, in a manuscript history of the Earls of Warwick, known as the Rous Roll, the work of John Rous the Warwick antiquary.

The period of Crown administration of Warwick Castle, which was to continue until 1547, witnessed two attempts at rebuilding. The first of these was by Richard III. The antiquary John Leland, who visited Warwick c.1540, wrote:

> The magnificent and stronge Castle of Warwicke ... is sett upon a huge Rocke of Stone, and hath 3 goodly Towres in the East Front of it. There is a fayre Towre on the North syde of it, and in this part of the Castle K. Rich. 3. pulled downe a peice of the Wall, and beganne and half finished a mighty Towre, or Strength, for to shoote out Gunnes.

This work was never to be completed and, even today, in Leland's words, 'it remaineth unfinished'. The second attempt at rebuilding Warwick was instigated by Henry VIII, and again this was noted by Leland:

> All the principall Lodginges of the Castle with an Hall and Chappell lye on the South Syde of the Castle, and the King doth much Cost in makinge Foundations in the Rockes to susteine that Syde of the Castle. For great peices fell out of the Rocke that sustained it.

Edward Plantagenet, Earl of Warwick since 1478, was executed in 1499, and for almost 50 years the earldom lay dormant. In 1547 the title was revived for the Dudley family, and John Dudley received it. He had been constable of Warwick Castle under its Crown administration since 1532, and with the title was granted its ownership and that of its land. In 1551 John Dudley was created Duke of Northumberland, and it was with this title that he was executed two years later for his attempt to place Lady Jane Grey upon the throne. Despite this his eldest surviving son, Ambrose, was permitted to succeed as Earl of Warwick in 1551, and the following year he received the castle and its estates. Ambrose Dudley died childless in 1590 with the castle becoming, once more, the possession of the sovereign, Elizabeth I, while the earldom again became dormant. The Queen never visited Warwick when it was in her possession, though she had done so in 1566 and again in 1572. On this latter occasion extra rooms had to

The prospect of it from London road on the south side of the Towne.

The Ground plott of WARWICK,

The Pryorye

be built to accommodate her retinue and herself, and a garden was created beside the Avon.

Despite the efforts made at Warwick for the visit of Queen Elizabeth, when the last Dudley Earl of Warwick died the castle was in a state of neglect. A survey of that year, 1590, tells of windows about to collapse, rain entering, and lead having been stolen from the roofs. Nothing was done to arrest this process of decay, and in 1601 Sir Fulke Greville the elder described Warwick as being 'the ruins of a house ... the wall down in many places hard to the ground; the roof open to all weathers ... in a short time there will be nothing left but a name of Warwick'. This same year the condition of the castle was reported on by the Royal Surveyor for Warwickshire, Thomas Dabridgcourt, who confirmed its sad state: 'there is such decay in the leads, tiles, boards, glass, iron and parts thereof, that it raineth in most parts of the castle ... a whole window in the great chamber is fallen down, and part of one of the towers, and many places of the outward wall ...'. Dabridgcourt's survey was so gloomy that he did not even trouble to give an estimate for repairing Warwick, merely contenting himself with a valuation of £470, this being the worth of the materials that would become available if the castle were demolished.

The final destruction of Warwick Castle was effectively prevented by Sir Fulke Greville the younger, and it is with his acquisition of the castle in 1604 that its modern history begins. In the years after 1604 Sir Fulke spent lavishly in rebuilding and restoring the ruined castle, where he intended, in the words of a contemporary, 'to keep a very great house'. What precisely it cost Sir Fulke to create his new Warwick is uncertain but it was recorded, some sixty years later, as being £20,000. An anonymous description of 1634, just six years after Greville's death, refers to 'a fayre and stately castle' and to the 'sumptuousness of the Building, with the richnesse of the Furniture, the pleasantnesse of the Seat ...'. Another of Sir Fulke's passions was for fine gardens, and we read of 'all kind of delightful and shady walkes, and Arbours, pleasant Groves, and wildernesses, fruitful Trees, delicious bowers, odoriferous Herbes, and fragrant Flowers ...'. Finally the writer tells us that Warwick was made 'thus rare and excellent at the great cost and charge of the worthy, and famous Knight, her late owner ...'.

Clearly Sir Fulke Greville had spent freely on Warwick and its gardens, and also furnished the interiors splendidly. Twenty-six years after Greville's death, the diarist John Evelyn visited Warwick and, though he thought the gardens could be 'much improved', wrote of the furniture as 'noble'. Inventories taken when Sir Fulke died reveal his particular love for fine tapestries, of which he had a large collection, though sadly almost nothing of this

5. Wenceslaus Hollar (1607-77), detail of an engraving of Warwick published in Sir William Dugdale's *Antiquities of Warwickshire*, 1656.

6. Samuel and Nathaniel Buck, *Warwick Castle from the North-east*, engraving, 1729.

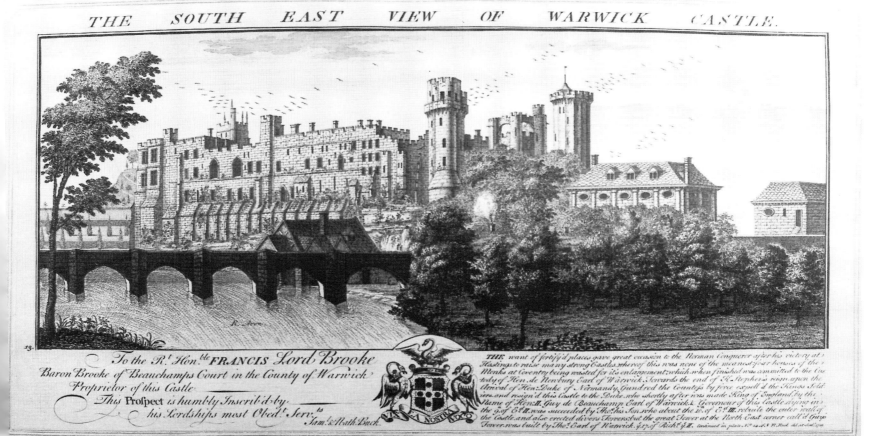

7. Samuel and Nathaniel Buck, *Warwick Castle from the South-east*, engraving, 1729.

remains at the castle today. Despite the many changes which have taken place in the centuries since his death, Warwick owes its survival entirely to Sir Fulke Greville, first Lord Brooke. Had he not persuaded James I to allow him its ownership there is little doubt it would have vanished forever.

The external appearance of Warwick Castle remained essentially unaltered in the years immediately following the death of the first Lord Brooke. We may obtain our first glimpse of its appearance during this period from an engraving of 1656 by the Bohemian artist, Wenceslaus Hollar [5]. This shows the castle with its principally Jacobean fenestration, but with a single Gothic arched window surviving from the medieval Warwick. On the left is the mound of the Norman castle which Sir Fulke Greville had had made into a climbing walk from which views could be obtained. Ascending the mound was a particular pleasure for 17th-century visitors to the castle, and almost all write of the delight it gave them. The topographer Thomas Baskerville, who came to Warwick in 1681, wrote of how he

> went up a fine winding walk set with herbs and various trees till we came to the top of the mount where grew

within a circle of laurel a Scottish fir tree ... I must confess it was very pleasant to behold the curiosities below ... the pleasant walks and curious knots, pretty flowers, arbours, and summer houses ... the site of a goodly vale and hills ... all together it is one of the best inland prospects our country doth afford.

Some seventy years after this account, Canaletto was to depict visitors to Warwick making this same walk to enjoy the view.

Thomas Baskerville not only enjoyed the gardens at Warwick but also remarked on the castle's 'noble rooms'; these were not, however, those created by Sir Fulke Greville. In the 1670s Robert Greville, fourth Baron Brooke, completely remodelled the principal interiors and created the state apartment which survives to the present day. He also introduced sash windows with glazing bars in the additional rooms he built to increase the castle's accommodation, and in 1667 a new coachhouse and stables was completed. Thus, by the close of the 17th century the medieval Warwick Castle had acquired much of the character of a Jacobean house, though with interiors from the Restoration period. This evolutionary development in the appearance of the castle was not affected by a severe fire in 1694, which destroyed over 400 buildings in the centre of Warwick. The destruction necessitated a programme of rebuilding, and radically altered the appearance of the town at the beginning of the 18th century.

The fourth Baron Brooke died in 1677, and only just lived to see his new interiors within Warwick Castle. His immediate successors, the fifth, sixth and seventh Barons, made few significant changes to Warwick, and it was essentially this castle which was inherited by Francis Greville, eighth Baron Brooke, in 1727. Its character at this time was well caught by Daniel Defoe who visited Warwick in 1724: 'the building is old, but several Times repair'd and beautify'd by its several Owners, and 'tis now a very agreeable place both within and without'. Two engravings, both from 1729, by Samuel and Nathaniel Buck show the castle that Defoe approved of and Francis Greville inherited. One [6] depicts the east front with its outer court of coachhouse, stables and pair of gates. The other [7] portrays Warwick's south front with its mixture of medieval, Jacobean and Restoration windows and, below the castle, the Avon and the medieval town bridge of Warwick.

The castle shown by the two Bucks was to be greatly changed in the course of the 18th century. The eighth Baron Brooke, after his return from the Grand Tour, began a programme of new building, of alterations and of landscaping at Warwick Castle. This work had only just commenced when Brooke was introduced to Canaletto, and in late 1747 or early 1748 he brought the artist to Warwick to begin work on the great series of paintings and drawings of his castle.

8. Warwick Castle from across Castle Park.

The Pictures

> 'In his pictures Canaletto combined nature and artistic licence with such skill that his works appear absolutely accurate to those who judge them only according to the principles of good sense ...'
>
> *Antonio Zanetti the Younger, 1771*

CANALETTO IS FIRST KNOWN to have been in London in May 1746, when his presence was recorded by the engraver and antiquary George Vertue. A year later, in 1747, he painted two views of the city for the second Duke of Richmond which were to be the finest things he was to do in England. The recommendation to the Duke, who had previously acquired the artist's Venetian work, had been arranged by the two men who had acted as Canaletto's agents, Owen McSwiney and Joseph Smith. By the time he painted these two views of London, Canaletto had also secured the patronage of Sir Hugh Smithson who, almost certainly, then introduced the artist to his wife's cousin, Lord Brooke. Within two years of his arrival in England, Canaletto had been commissioned to visit Warwick and to begin painting pictures of its castle.

Canaletto's first view of Warwick Castle would probably have been from the old Banbury road, as he travelled north from London in the spring of 1748. At this date the road from Banbury to Warwick lay across what was later to become a part of the castle's park, while the road itself was moved to the east. This new road, opened in 1792, required the building of a second bridge over the Avon which is still in use today. These events were not, however, to take place until the end of the 18th century, and in Canaletto's time the now ruined Great Bridge at the castle itself, which collapsed in 1795, formed the only river crossing, with all traffic from the south being compelled to use it. Thus Canaletto's first sight of Warwick would have been from across the valley of the Avon and he would have seen the castle rather as in the engraving by Hollar [5]. Today, though this view is largely obscured by trees, one may still catch something of the effect it must have had on him [8]. It was this dramatic aspect of the castle's south front that the artist first depicted.

Canaletto portrayed Warwick, principally the castle but also, briefly and exquisitely, the town, on three distinct occasions. The first two of these were close together, with the third

9. Canaletto, *Warwick Castle: the South Front*, 1748. Oil on canvas, 42 x 71 cm. Private Collection, New York.

separated by a period of some three years. In all, he executed five oil paintings and five pen drawings, the latter enhanced with washes of grey colour.

The first of Canaletto's pictures of Warwick is the smallest of the paintings he created. It shows the castle in the light of the early morning, when its southern aspect is seen to best advantage [9]. In this work the great south face looks old and stained, with the windows appearing as they did in the earlier view by the brothers Buck, in 1729 [7]. On the right of the picture is the Great Bridge, over which Canaletto himself travelled, with the roofs of Warwick and the spire of St Nicholas' church beyond. Below the mass of Caesar's Tower is the castle mill and weir. On the left of the painting there are two bridges, neither of which survives today; that nearest the castle and built of wood gave access to Castle Meadow, the island which divides the Avon at Warwick, while the further bridge from the castle, built of stone, led into Castle Park. The former was pulled down in 1753, while the latter collapsed in a flood of 1824. Following the line of the two bridges into the picture, one comes to the old castle mound and, below this, work is in progress to remove the formal gardens created by Sir Fulke Greville some 140 years before. This work was part of Capability Brown's landscaping of the castle grounds, and Canaletto has even included a lean-to erected for the labourers and their tools.

The mound itself, the 'winding walk' up which figures are ascending, is topped by a single Scots pine tree.

In his first painting of the castle, Canaletto showed it as yet little changed by Lord Brooke's improvements but, probably as a result of this first visit and what he may have heard of Brooke's plans, he also painted a large canvas of a transformed Warwick [10]. This picture views the castle from Castle Meadow, much closer, and Canaletto shows the summit of the further of the great towers, Guy's, as visible, even though this is impossible from the island (although it can be seen from the Avon's far bank). The old Tudor mill has been swept away, as has the weir, and a barge, possibly Brooke's 'pleasure boat', is shown upon the river. In place of the old stained castle face with its assortment of windows shown in his first picture [9], Warwick now has a regular fenestration or window arrangement with sashes and glazing bars. All signs of work on the gardens have gone and fully grown trees have appeared beside the Avon and mound. The Scots pine on the mound's summit was originally included by the artist, but he then painted it out as if the intention had been to fell it. In fact the tree remained until 1844, when it was blown down in a storm.

This second painting by Canaletto was probably made, at least in part, to give Lord Brooke an impression of how the castle would appear after his schemes for its improvement had been

The Pictures

carried out. In the event, such things as the weir and mill were to remain, though the latter was rebuilt in 1767. That Brooke did indeed introduce further sash windows to the castle is clear, as in 1754 the poet Thomas Gray wrote that he had 'sash'd the great apartment', by which Gray meant the principal interiors. These two pictures reveal Warwick Castle as it was when Canaletto first saw it, and how he envisaged it would look when the plans of Brooke and Capability Brown had been carried out.

Our earliest documentation for Canaletto's depictions of Warwick is the first of four payments to the artist in Lord Brooke's account at Hoare's Bank in London. This first payment, dated 19 July 1748, is to 'Sigr. Canall' for £58 [12] and is probably for the first two paintings, the larger costing more than the smaller. The date establishes that Canaletto first visited Warwick in late 1747 or early 1748.

The next sum of money paid to Canaletto does not appear in Lord Brooke's private bank account but in the accounts kept for his estates. This was the work of his own receivers of rents. On 28 July 1748 one such receiver, Samuel Dixon, records a payment of 10 guineas which the estate accounts volume describes as for 'Drawings' [15]. This is almost certainly a mistake since Canaletto himself wrote out a receipt for the money in which he refers to only one work [16]. This receipt is the only known document in the artist's own hand referring to his work at Warwick. The precise meaning of Canaletto's Italian words is uncertain but they could be translated as reading: 'As of 28 July 1748 London Received I Giovanni Antonio Canal from the agent of the most excellent My Lord Brooke. Ten guineas, and this for the price of a small picture by me depicted with the view of the castle of the said My Lord'. Very few original documents in Canaletto's own handwriting are known, so the survival of this one is of great importance.

The payment of 10 guineas is for Canaletto's only drawing of Warwick Castle's south front [11]. This drawing is superficially close to the painting [9] but is very different from the vision of the improved Warwick [10]. In the drawing Canaletto has included more figures than in his first painting, such as that of the lady standing at the entrance to the stone bridge on the left. He has also shown an increased number of sash windows in the castle, and in particular elaborate Gothic sash window frames for the principal drawing room in the centre of the south face. It is probable that, after seeing Warwick for the painting [9], Canaletto came again after changes to the windows had been made. The drawing shows work on the landscaping of the park as in the earlier picture.

Canaletto's next portrayal of Warwick, another large oil painting, dates from the end of 1748 [13]. Once again, there is a

10. Canaletto, *Warwick Castle: the South Front*, 1748. Oil on canvas, 75 x 120.5 cm. Thyssen-Bornemisza Collection, Lugano.

11. Canaletto, *Warwick Castle: the South Front*. 1748. Pen and brown ink with grey wash, 31.7 x 57.8 cm. Private Collection.

The Rt. Honble. ye Earl Brooke — Dr.

1748

			£	s	d
May 30	To himself	1	200	—	
31	To Do.	1	1370		
June 10	To Thursby Dixon	1	180		
17	To Clarke & Sedgwick	1	100		
21	To himself	1	500		
July 19	To Sigr. Canall	1	58		
30	To £1000 East India Bond & Int. at 1¾ pr. Ct. &c.	1	1023	15	9
Octr. 4	To Fred: Nyssen	1	100		
10	Letty Carver	1	31	10	
17	To Jos. Woodhouse	1	200		
Novr. 1	To Rt. Kempton for acy. Fancy to Michs. last	1	10		
3	To Jos. Woodhouse	1	200		
14	To Edwd. Croft	1	100		
15	To Jos. Woodhouse	1	200		
Decr. 26	To Do.	1	100		
			300		

The Pictures

payment for this in Lord Brooke's bank account when, on 3 March 1748, £31 10s. (30 gs.) was paid to 'Sigr. G. Anto Canale' [21]. At this time (and until 1751) the year ended on 25 March so this payment was made later than the other two of 1748.

The painting [13] is the last and grandest of Canaletto's depictions of Warwick's south front, with many figures and even swans upon the river. Like the drawing [11], this picture shows the new Gothic-style windows which Lord Brooke had introduced to the castle's Cedar Drawing Room; these stand out in brilliant white from the stonework [14]. These new windows were noted by Philip Yorke, heir to the Earldom of Hardwicke, who visited Warwick in August 1748, and wrote:

> Warwick castle ... being in perfect good order and improving every year under the care of its present owner, Earl Brooke ... the state apartments, consisting of 5 well-proportioned lofty rooms, the largest of which is wainscoted with cedar; the windows of it are new, but made in the Gothic style and very pretty.

Yorke also mentions the walk across the bridges shown by Canaletto: 'The view from the windows over the town of Warwick, the river, and the park on the opposite side, to which you cross by a wooden bridge, and of the distant country is very grand and very striking'. Like his earlier painting [9] this later one has, on the right, the bridge and roofs of the town of Warwick and the spire of St Nicholas' church, while on the left figures ascend the castle mound. Canaletto was the first artist to depict this activity, which delighted the 18th-century visitor to Warwick as much as it had those of the 17th century. Like others before him, Yorke made the climb: 'Round the court of the castle is a steep green slope ... a high mount cut into slopes, and a seat at the top of which there is a very extensive prospect'. This seat, painted white, is shown by Canaletto surrounding the Scots pine tree. Presumably the artist himself ascended the mound, though he has left us no drawings or paintings of what he saw. The appearance of Warwick from the bank of the Avon farthest from the castle, and from where Canaletto studied it, is now heavily obscured by trees, but one may still glimpse something of the view he was to depict so memorably [20]. This is still more true from Castle Meadow [41].

The three paintings and the drawing [9, 10, 11 & 13] are the result of Lord Brooke's initial patronage of Canaletto; they were not, however, to be the end of the artist's involvement with Warwick. Before considering Brooke's second patronage of the artist and the paintings and drawings this produced, it is perhaps worth reflecting on the manner in which Canaletto approached a commission to depict scenes such as those of Warwick Castle.

12. Detail of Hoare's Bank ledger showing first Earl Brooke's account, 1748.

13. Canaletto, *Warwick Castle: the South Front*, 1748(9). Oil on canvas, 72.4 x 120.5 cm. Paul Mellon Collection, Upperville, Virginia.

14. Detail of plate 13.

Paid Mr Hutchins the Attorney in the Country his own & the Commissioner's Fees at that Commission .... 57 . 9 . —
Paid Mr Whitlock his Bill for Herringston Recovery and other Matters .... 20 . 5 . —
Paid Charges to the Sheriffs Officer on taking Possession of Kitchen's House .... 2 . 3 . 4
Paid the Officer for breaking open the Door on taking possession and putting on a Lock .... 6 . 6
The Bill for passing the Leweston Act .... 177 . 10 . —
A Bill for Law Business and Charges on Several Acco.ts from Lady day 1748 to this time .... 97 . 15 . —

10. **Cash paid to Lord Brooke's Order, and to Mr Hoare on his Lordships Acco.t**

May 28 Paid L.d Brooke's Dr.t of this date to Mr Tomkins Dew, being for Change out of Col.l Mardours Bank Notes, paid to his Lordship at Hiffindon .... 31 . 4 . 6
To Seign.r Canal for his Drawings of Warwick Castle .... 10 . 10 . —
To the Clerks at Mr Hoare's on his Lordship's Settling his Accounts there .... 5 . 5 . —
For Several other payments as p.r paper of Particulars .... 9 . 15 . 10
March 23 Paid Mr Hoare .... 287 . 17 . 6

23 March 1748
This Account is just & true in all Particulars
to y.e best of my knowledge, & the Vouchers answer to it
Sam.l Dixon

Allowed
Brooke.

Total Discharge

15. Detail of a folio from the first Earl Brooke's estate account ledgers, 1748. Greville Archive, Warwick County Record Office.

THE PICTURES

Canaletto, it should be remembered, was not a topographical artist. This is not to say that he was not concerned with accurately depicting what he saw, but that he was, first and foremost, an artist whose aim was the creation of a work of art. To understand this one must appreciate his method of working. None of Canaletto's paintings and drawings of Warwick would have been done at the castle itself—all would have been produced at his London studio in what was then Silver Street (now Beak Street). When he arrived at Warwick, Canaletto would have been carrying sketchbooks with pages measuring some four by eight inches. On the pages of these books he would have made numerous sketches or drawings of the castle, noting particular architectural features

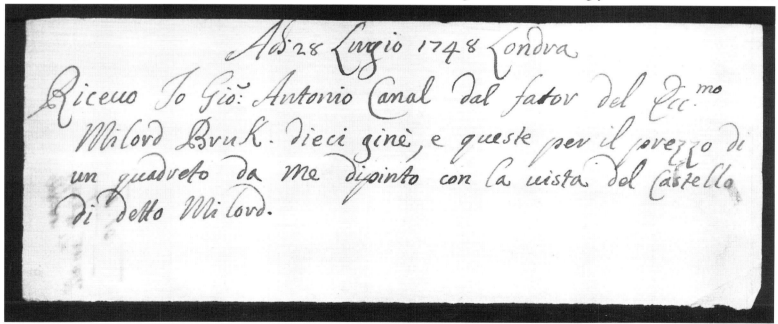

16. Voucher in Canaletto's own handwriting. The first Earl Brooke's estate account vouchers, 1748.
Greville Archive, Warwick County Record Office.

17. Canaletto, *Warwick Castle: the East Front from the Outer Court*, 1752. Oil on canvas, 73 × 122 cm. Birmingham Museum and Art Gallery.

18 & 19. Detail of plate 17.

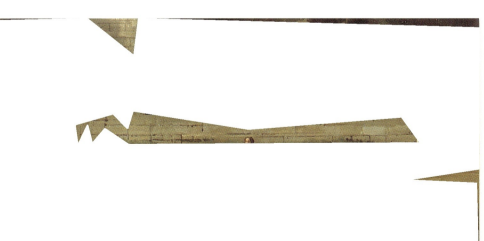

THE PICTURES

20. Warwick Castle: the south front.

and details such as windows, roofs and towers. He would also have recorded in words such things as materials used and their colours. Canaletto would then have returned to his studio with these sketches and notes, to begin work on his paintings and drawings. Unfortunately none of his preliminary sketches of Warwick are known to have survived. Once in the studio, he would have relied on his artist's sense of the pictorial, his painter's eye and hand, to create the picture. It is, therefore, meaningless to ask if Canaletto's paintings show Warwick exactly as it was; to do so is to miss the point of his art. Canaletto's works are not, in a simple sense, reality; yet neither are they wholly divorced from it. Rather they are the product of a great artist's technique and vision of how Warwick should be seen. In this sense they surpass the castle itself.

The payment Lord Brooke made to Canaletto at the close of 1748 [21] was, as far as is known, the last contact between them for some three years. During this time the artist returned to Venice for about eight months, but was back in England by the summer of 1751. Brooke had continued his alterations to Warwick and its park and, in late 1751 or early 1752, he called Canaletto to visit the castle once more. We know this because on 24 March 1752 the sum of £33 12s. (32 gs.) was paid to 'Sigr. Canaletti' by him [22].

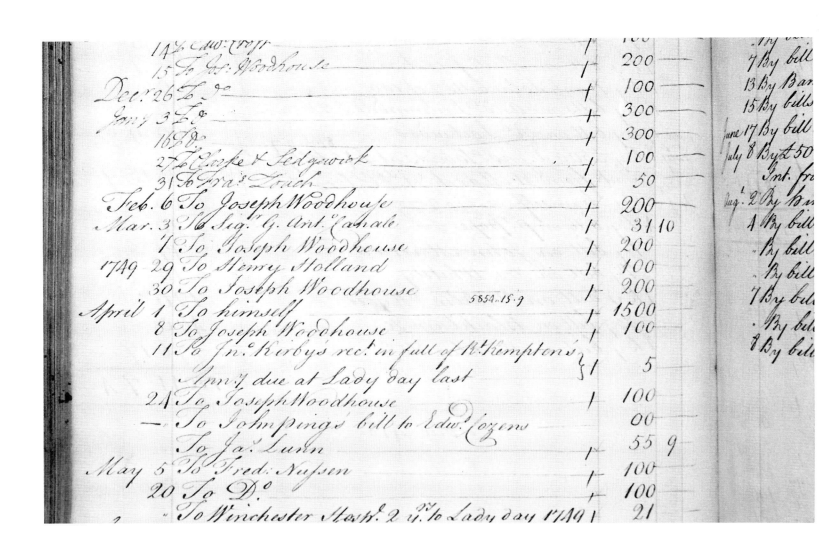

21. Detail of Hoare's Bank ledger showing first Earl Brooke's account, 1748(9).

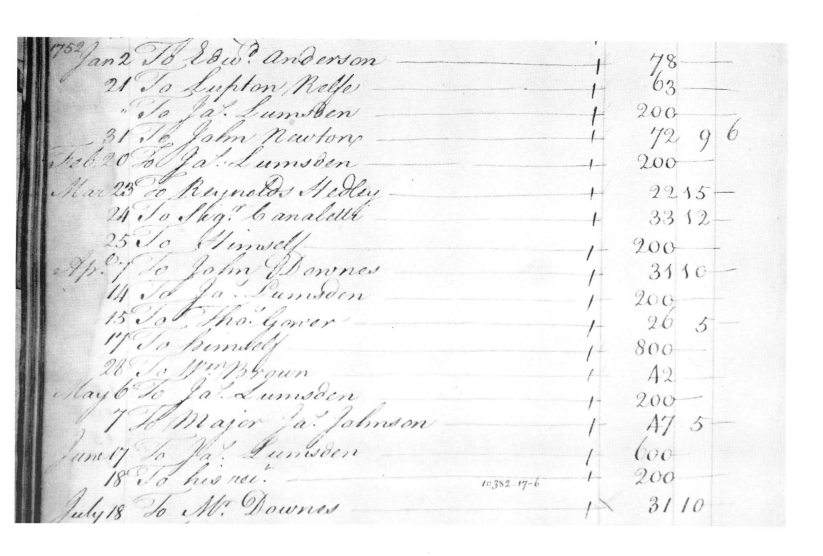

22. Detail of Hoare's Bank ledger showing first Earl Brooke's account, 1752.

23. Canaletto, *Warwick Castle: the East Front from the Courtyard*, 1752. Oil on canvas, 75 x 122 cm. Birmingham Museum and Art Gallery.

24. Detail of plate 23.

This must have been for one of the two large paintings of Warwick's east front and may be for that which showed the castle from what was then the outer courtyard [17]. When Canaletto came to Warwick, the stables built in 1667 were still in use, and the corner of the building may be seen at the extreme left of his painting. The stables were themselves linked, by a wall, to the porter's lodge and pair of gates visible on the right of the canvas. This old arrangement may be seen on the engraving of 1729 by the brothers Buck [6].

Lord Brooke's cousin Elizabeth, Duchess of Northumberland, visited Warwick at this time and gave the following account of it:

> Warwick, which is a handsome but a very idle Town, no Trade being carry'd on there. The Castle is quite at the end of it. When you enter the first Court, the Stables are on the left hand, which are built in a horrid stile & the Coach Houses in front. Soon after you turn to the right through a Gateway into the inner Court, having on yr. right hand Guy's Tower & the Mount, wch. has been the Keep of the Castle, & on the left Caesar's Tower.

For almost the entire 18th century the carriage drive at Warwick lay along the castle's moat, directly below the towers and walls of the east front. It led up from the town's Mill Street, which itself began from the bridge over the Avon. Canaletto must have arrived at the castle by this route, and after driving along the moat, his coach would have turned through the gates and into Warwick's outer and inner courtyards.

Canaletto's painting of the east front [17] is, perhaps, the most familiar of all his views of Warwick Castle with its great towers—Caesar's on the left, Guy's on the right. Between the central gatehouse and barbican and Caesar's Tower are the windows of what was then the castle's brewhouse and laundry. On the right of the picture Canaletto provides a glimpse of the medieval town of Warwick, which at that time came almost to the edge of the castle's moat [18]. These cottages were to be demolished towards the end of the 18th century when the castle grounds were extended. Although the figures Canaletto shows are his invention, intended to animate the scene and give the effect of those taking their ease amidst the splendours of Warwick, some, such as the porter in his livery, did exist and could have been sketched by the artist. In the centre of the painting is one of his most beautiful figure arrangements [19]. As with Canaletto's views of the south front, that of the east front is depicted by him in the light of early morning, since it is this which shows Warwick to best advantage.

Warwick Castle's outer courtyard, with its 17th-century stables, was progressively destroyed in the latter half of the 18th century when, with the creation of a new porter's lodge and

25. Warwick Castle: the east front.

carriage drive, the east front took on much of the appearance which survives to the present day. In all his paintings and drawings of Warwick, Canaletto uses a raised viewpoint. Despite this, and changes to the castle grounds, after some two and a half centuries his dramatic vision of Warwick may still be experienced [25 & 31].

Shortly after Canaletto completed his first painting of Warwick's east front, he painted another picture showing the same feature but from the other side—that is, from the castle's principal courtyard or inner court [23]. He also created a pair of drawings of the same two sides of the east front to complement the paintings [26 & 29]. The final payment in Lord Brooke's account to 'Antonio Canal' of 27 July 1752 for £50 [27] may well be for this last painting and the pair of drawings. The painting [23] shows, on the extreme right, a corner of the castle's domestic apartments with their sash windows and glazing bars. In the arch at the base of the gatehouse, Canaletto has shown the spire of St Nicholas' church, while to the right a pair of young trees in supporting frames must be part of Brown's landscaping of the courtyard [24]. Above the outer wall projects the chimney of the castle's laundry, showing how closely Canaletto had observed and noted the details of the building, while below, the swirling dresses of the women and gestures of the men enliven the scene. Though the elegance of the gentlemen and their ladies may now be missing, the view itself is little changed [28].

Capability Brown's landscaping at Warwick was not completed until after Canaletto had left England forever and he never saw the castle's courtyard with its present oval lawn. The east front itself, however, still looks much as the artist saw it. All of Canaletto's depictions of Warwick's eastern aspect show it with the light falling from the left, but while for the view from the outer court [17] this effect is visible in the morning, for that view from the courtyard it may only be seen in the afternoon [23]. Both of these lightings correspond to the times Canaletto has shown indicated by the single hand of the castle clock.

In addition to his views of the castle, Canaletto also made two drawings of the town of Warwick itself which are themselves entire works of art. One of these [30] shows the view of St Mary's church from Church Street, while the other is a prospect of the town from the gardens of Warwick Priory [33]. The existence of these two drawings, which again would have been made from preliminary sketches taken on the spot, shows that while studying the castle, Canaletto also explored the town of Warwick.

From the existence of the drawing [30] it is clear that Canaletto walked from the castle itself up Castle Street in the direction

26. Canaletto, *Warwick Castle: the East Front from the Outer Court*, 1752. Pen and brown ink with grey wash, 31.6 x 56.2 cm. Metropolitan Museum of Art, New York, Robert Lehman Collection.

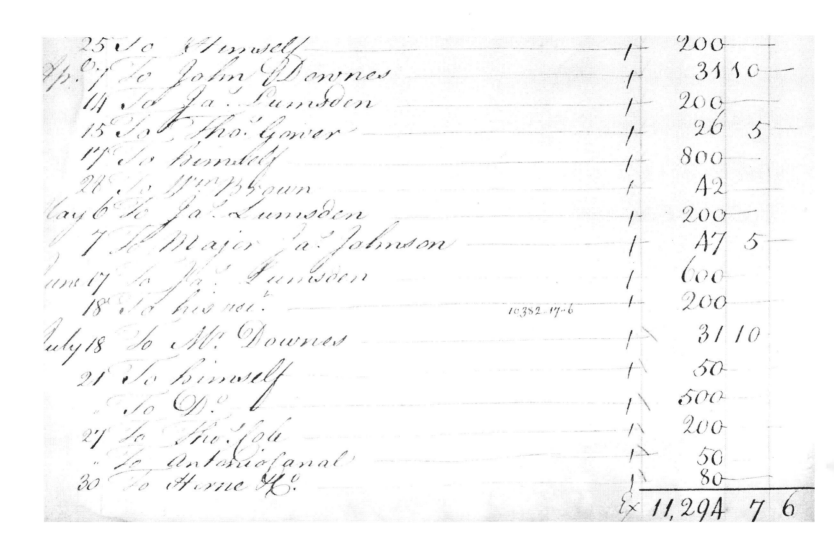

27. Detail of Hoare's Bank ledger showing first Earl Brooke's account, 1752.

28. Warwick Castle: the east front from the courtyard.

29. Canaletto, *Warwick Castle: the East Front from the Courtyard*, 1752. Pen and brown ink with grey wash, 31.7 x 57.1 cm. J. Paul Getty Museum, Malibu, California.

30. Canaletto, *St Mary's Church and Church Street, Warwick*, 1748 or 1752. Pen and brown ink with grey wash, 35.4 x 28.2 cm. British Museum.

of St Mary's church. A map of Warwick in the late 18th century enables us to follow the route the artist would have taken [32]. Canaletto must have been struck by the sight of the church which he glimpsed between buildings constructed as part of the rebuilding of Warwick after the fire of 1694. The artist's view of St Mary's from this point was actually crossed by the town's High Street but Canaletto has simply omitted this, giving an uninterrupted prospect of the church and of Church Street which he has widened. The building on the right of the drawing, with its classical balustrade and finials, is the new Court House designed by the Warwick architect Francis Smith. Church Street, Warwick, is one of the least altered of all Canaletto's English scenes and, even today, it is still possible to see much of the view Canaletto was struck by over two centuries ago [34]. He labelled the drawing, somewhat quaintly, *Ingresso nella Piazza de Varik* — Entrance in the Square of Warwick.

After making his sketch of the view of St Mary's, Canaletto must have crossed the High Street and continued up Church Street past the church, and along Sheep Street to the Priory. This house, built in the reign of Elizabeth I, was pulled down in 1925. What caused Canaletto to visit the Priory is uncertain as no depictions of it by him are known. It may be that he wished to study the

31. Warwick Castle: the east front.

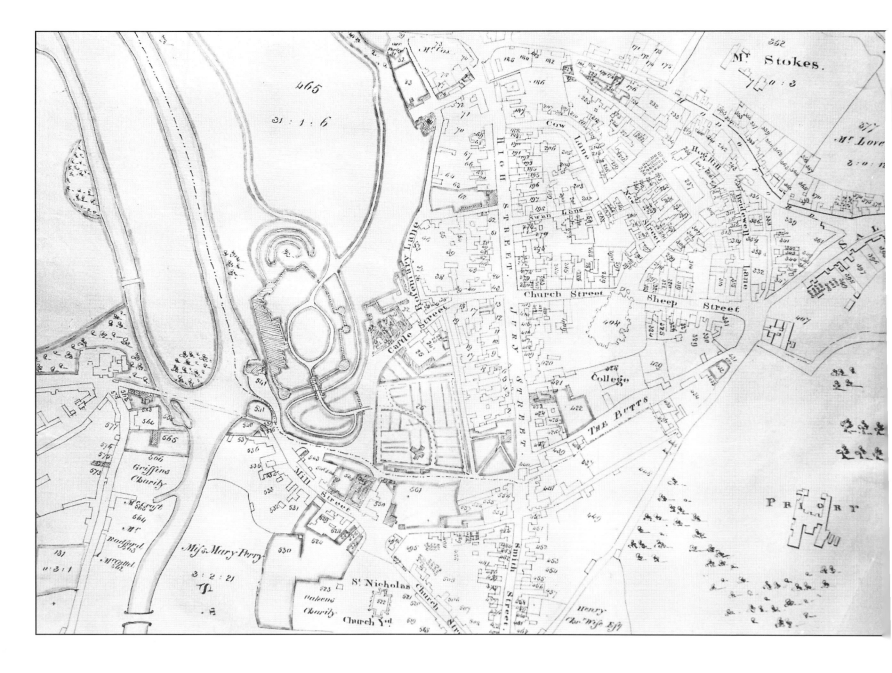

33. Canaletto, *The Town and Castle of Warwick seen from the Gardens of the Priory*, 1748 or 1752. Pen and brown ink with grey wash, 35.5 x 92 cm. Yale Center for British Art, New Haven, Connecticut.

2. *(left)* Detail of the plan of Warwick by Matthias Baker, 1788. Greville Archive, Warwick County Record Office.

34. St Mary's church and Church Street, Warwick.

35. The town and castle of Warwick from Priory Park.

east front of the castle as part of a prospect of the town of Warwick itself.

During the early years of the 18th century the owner of the Priory, Henry Wise, had formal gardens laid out facing Warwick, and these have been included by Canaletto in his picture [33]. The drawing is dominated on the right by the tower of St Mary's church, itself rebuilt following the Warwick fire, while in the centre is the castle's east front, to the left of which lies the tower of the town's east gate and, at the extreme left of the drawing, the spire of St Nicholas' church. Canaletto always had a liking for a vista which included a line of spires and towers, as may be seen in many of his views of London. Nothing now remains of the gardens the artist saw, but one may still appreciate something of the view he sketched [35]. Precisely why Canaletto made these two elaborate drawings of Warwick is uncertain. There is no evidence that he undertook them for Lord Brooke, so the exact reason for their creation remains a mystery. With these last two works, Canaletto completed what had been a remarkable relationship between a great 18th-century Venetian artist and a provincial English town and its castle.

The Story

> 'Canaletto once resided at the Castle, under the patronage of the late Earl of Warwick, who amongst other works employed him in painting views of the Castle.'
>
> *William Field, 1815*

THE PAYMENT TO CANALETTO of £50 by Lord Brooke on 27 July 1752 is the last known communication between them. There is no evidence that Canaletto ever visited Warwick again and, though Brooke continued his works at the castle, the artist was never again called upon to depict them. The 10 works of art which resulted from the relationship between Canaletto and his patron (and Brooke was to be one of the artist's most loyal patrons during his time in England) are unique in the history of art: a series of views of one of England's great historic buildings, and its setting, by a master scenic painter.

After the completion of his work for Lord Brooke, Canaletto remained in England for some three years, departing for Italy in either 1755 or 1756. In all he resided in London for about nine years, and the majority of his paintings and drawings done during this period are views of the capital and places adjacent to it. Apart from Warwick the only other country houses he depicted are Badminton House and Alnwick Castle. Sadly, the English collectors who had desired his paintings of Venice so avidly had little interest in acquiring his views of their own country.

On his return to Venice, Canaletto, by then aged 60, continued to produce a few pictures of the city, but the days of English noblemen touring Europe and demanding his work were gone forever. In 1762 his old patron and agent, Joseph Smith, sold much of his great collection of the artist's works to George III, and thus they entered the royal collection of which they still form a part. The hundreds of other paintings and drawings made by Canaletto are now found throughout the public and private art collections of the world.

When Canaletto first arrived in England, George Vertue observed that he was by then already 'easy in his fortune', implying that he was rich from the sales of his paintings of Venice. If this was true then what became of the money is a mystery, since on his death he left very little. He never married and of his private life almost nothing is known. Canaletto died through inflammation of the bladder and the resultant fever on 19 April 1768. He was 70 years old and maintained his skill as a draughtsman to the end,

shown by the drawing he made in 1766, on which he proudly wrote that it had been done 'Cenzza Ochiali'—without spectacles.

After his last commissions to Canaletto, Lord Brooke continued his improvements at Warwick, though he never again acquired major pictures of the castle. In 1759 the family of Rich, which had been Earls of Warwick since 1618, died out, and Brooke at once sought and received this title from George II. In this way the Earldom of Warwick and ownership of the castle were reunited after an interval of 169 years. Brooke himself greatly preferred the title Earl of Warwick and wished to be known as such. Later, the title of Lord Brooke became that taken by the eldest son of the earl.

In the years following his patronage of Canaletto and, most pronouncedly, in those following his receiving the title of Lord Warwick, Francis Greville chose to introduce the 18th-century's Gothic taste to the castle. In 1765 he built a new set of interiors which included what he called the 'Great Dining Room'. Warwick had this placed in the centre of the castle's residential apartment, something which Canaletto never depicted as viewed from the courtyard. He had a local painter, John Pye, make a painting of this in imitation of the Venetian artist [36]. The picture is the same size as Canaletto's small view of Warwick's south front [9] and, framed identically, it must have been intended to hang as a companion to it. After the building of the Great Dining Room, Lord Warwick had towers placed on the mound, the mill rebuilt in the Gothic style and new stables completed shortly before his death in 1773. It was inevitable that this process of change would be carried on by the earl's descendants. Nevertheless, after two and a half centuries the castle is still intrinsically and recognisably that which Canaletto saw.

Lord Brooke, or as he was later to become, Lord Warwick, did not place Canaletto's paintings and drawings at the castle but almost certainly kept them in his London home. At the time Canaletto worked for him, Brooke lived in Grosvenor Square, though he was later to have other London residences. In the event the set of five paintings and three drawings did not remain together for long. The drawing of the south front of Warwick Castle [11] was taken to Calke Abbey in Derbyshire by Brooke's eldest daughter, Frances, probably in 1764 when she married the abbey's owner, Sir Henry Harpur. On her death, in 1825, it was returned to her nephew, Henry Richard Greville, third Earl of Warwick. With the first earl's death, in 1773, ownership of the Canaletto pictures, like that of the castle, passed to his eldest son, George, second Earl of Warwick. He or his brother Charles then gave the two drawings [26 & 29] to the water-colourist Paul Sandby, who himself painted many views of Warwick Castle. Following Sandby's death in 1809 they were sold, and are now in American museums.

36. John Pye (1745-?74), *Warwick Castle: the Courtyard and Residential Apartment*, 1765. Oil on canvas, 41 x 71 cm. Private Collection.

37 & 38. Warwick Castle: the Red Room hung with the Canalettos, 1950.

As his father had done, the second earl kept Canaletto's five paintings in London. In 1772 he married Georgiana Peachy, the daughter of Sir James Peachy, first Baron Selsey. She was to die only a year after their marriage, yet one of the Canalettos [13] passed into Lord Selsey's collection, either as a gift from his son-in-law or perhaps in exchange for another picture. In this way the set of five paintings was broken, with one leaving the collection of the Earls of Warwick never to return; it is now in the Paul Mellon Collection. When the second earl died suddenly, in 1816, the four remaining pictures were hanging at his London house in Green Street.

The second Earl of Warwick was succeeded by his son, Henry, who as third earl brought the four paintings from London to hang at Warwick Castle in about 1845, almost 100 years after they were painted. Once at Warwick the pictures were first placed in the castle's billiard room, two of them later being moved to the sitting rooms. In 1871 Warwick Castle suffered a severe fire and the architect Anthony Salvin, who was responsible for the restoration, created an interior which the Greville family used as a breakfast room. This became the Canalettos' permanent home. In the Victorian age pictures were hung one above the other and very close together, so Canaletto's paintings would have formed only part of a large picture arrangement.

For much of its long history, Warwick Castle has been visited by travellers and tourists. During the 19th and 20th centuries, the numbers of such visitors gradually increased, though almost none saw the Canalettos, as they were hung in a room that was closed to them. In 1950 the seventh Earl of Warwick allowed the four paintings and the drawing by Canaletto, the painting by Pye, and a large view of Venice to be moved to the castle's Red Room. Until the following year, they were on public display at Warwick for the first time [37 & 38]. At the close of 1951 the pictures were taken back to their normal home at the castle, and were rarely shown to the public again.

In 1969 ownership of Warwick Castle and of the Canalettos passed to the seventh earl's son, David Lord Brooke, who succeeded his father as the eighth Earl of Warwick in 1984. In 1977, eight years after they were passed to him, the great-great-great-great-great-grandson of the Greville who had commissioned them sold the four paintings which remained in the family's collection. The small painting [9] is now with an American private collector, while the larger idealised view [10] entered the Thyssen-Bournemiza Collection. The two paintings of Warwick's east front [17 & 23] remained in England, being acquired by the Birmingham Museum and Art Gallery.

At the time of the sale, the surviving documents relating to

39. Signature of the first Earl Brooke.

40. Signature of Canaletto.

the pictures, the payments to the artist and his receipt for one of them, had yet to be identified. The discovery of these papers has made it possible to understand and appreciate more fully the scale of the first Earl Brooke's patronage of Canaletto and the great art which resulted. For anyone fortunate enough to have the opportunity of making a detailed study of Canaletto's paintings and drawings of Warwick and, perhaps, coming upon the receipt he drew up [16], the sensation is immediate. Unfolding this small slip of paper and realising it is in the artist's writing, one is linked to him and to the art he created. Today, though all Canaletto's works have left Warwick and his paintings and drawings are scattered, they may still be found, seen and enjoyed. In this way one may reach back, if only momentarily, to join again with Lord Brooke, his artist, his castle, and with the glory of Canaletto at Warwick.

41. Warwick Castle: the south front.

Bibliography

Baskerville, Thomas, Portland MSS. Historical MSS. Comm. (1902)

Beaumont, George, and Disney, Henry, *A New Tour thro' England performed in the summers of 1765, 1766, & 1767* (1768)

Buttery, David, 'Canaletto at Warwick' in *The Burlington Magazine* (July 1987)

Buttery, David, 'Canaletto's Patron' in *Apollo* (January 1992)

Cokayne, George Edward, *The Complete Peerage*, Vol. II (1912)

Constable, W. G., *Canaletto*, third edition revised and with supplement by J. G. Links (1989)

Cooke, Henry T., *A Guide to Warwick with its Castle & Surroundings* (c.1890)

Cooke, Henry T., *Present State of the Castle* (1846)

Defoe, Daniel, *A Tour thro' the whole island of Great Britain ... by a Gentleman* (1724-25)

Dugdale, Sir William, *Antiquities of Warwickshire* (1656)

Evelyn, John, *The Diary of John Evelyn*, Vol. III (1955)

Farr, Michael W., 'The Castle and Castle Estate in Warwick' in *The Victoria History of the County of Warwick*, Vol. VIII (1969)

Field, William, *An Historical and Descriptive Account of the Town and Castle of Warwick* (1815)

Gray, Thomas, *Correspondence*, Vol. I (1935)

Hartford, Frances, Countess of, *Correspondence between Frances Countess of Hartford and Henrietta Louisa Countess of Pomfret between the years 1738 and 1741* (1805)

Jacques, David, 'Capability Brown at Warwick Castle' in *Country Life* (22 February 1979)

Leland, John, *The Itinerary of John Leland* (1745)

Links, J. G., *Canaletto* (1982)

Metropolitan Museum of Art, New York, *Catalogue of the Canaletto Exhibition* (1989)

Northumberland, Elizabeth Duchess of, *The Diaries of a Duchess* (1926)

Norwich, a Captain, a Lieutenant, and an Ancient of the Military Company of, *A Short Survey of twenty-six counties observed in a seven weeks Journey*, Stuart series, VII (1904)

Pococke, Richard, *The Travels through England*, Camden Society second series, 44 (1889)

Rebholz, Ronald A., *The Life of Fulke Greville, first Lord Brooke* (1971)

Strider, Robert E. L., *Robert Greville, Lord Brooke* (1958)

Vertue, George, *Notebooks*, Walpole Society Vol. XXII (1933-34)

Walpole, Horace, *Correspondence*, Vol. 17 (1955)

Yorke, Philip, *Journal*, Bedford Historical Record Society (1968)

The Subscribers

I am grateful to Warwick Castle, and the following who provide their services to it, for each subscribing to 50 copies of this book.

Warwick Castle Ltd.
Ascough & Associates, Consultant Civil and Structural Engineers.
John Austin & Partners, Chartered Quantity Surveyors.
Crosbee & Atkins, The Builders.
Databuild, Building Technologists.
N. W. Dixon, Lighting Specialists and Electrical Contractors.
Leader Communications Ltd., Public Relations and Marketing Consultants.
Rodney Melville & Partners, Chartered Architects.
Millward Brown International Market Research.
Wragg Bros. Ltd., Masonry Contractors, Specialists in Stonework Restoration.